AS A WOMAN THINKS
Large Print Edition
BY
JAMES ALLEN &
JANICE DEMANO

Mind is the Master power
that moulds and makes,
And Woman is Mind, and
evermore she takes,
The tool of Thought, and,
shaping what she wills,
Brings forth a thousand joys,
a thousand ills.
She thinks in secret and
it comes to pass,
Environment is but
her looking glass.

Janice and Mel's
Life Transformation Publishing
© 2013 Janice Demano

ISBN: 978-0-9825830-7-4

Janice & Mel's
Life Transformation Publishing
133 Slazing Rd
Potosi, WI 53820
melwaller@gmail.com
www.lifetransformationpublishing.com

Specializing in Transforming Lives!

CONTENTS

FOREWORD

THIS little volume (the result of medita-
tion and experience) is not intended as
an exhaustive treatise on the much written upon subject of the power of thought.
It is suggestive rather than explanatory,
its object being to stimulate men and
women to the discovery and perception
of the truth that--

"They themselves are makers of themselves."

by virtue of the thoughts, which they
choose and encourage; that mind is the
master weaver, both of the inner garment
of character and the outer garment of
circumstance, and that, as they may have
before woven in ignorance and pain they
may now weave in enlightenment and
happiness.

JAMES ALLEN.
BROAD PARK AVENUE,
ILFRACOMBE, ENGLAND

Introduction

Thoughts are indeed powerful and can influence us in both positive and negative ways. In times past, it was commonplace for man to refer to both men and women. And as women we can surely understand this, but how much more powerful the words are that are written directly for the feminine in us. So I have rewritten this great work originally titled, As a Man Thinketh by James Allen and using feminine pronouns rather than masculine along with modern English present this work to the women of the world. May you each be empowered by the truths contained within.

Janice Demano
Philippines

AS A WOMAN THINKS

THOUGHT AND CHARACTER

THE aphorism, "As a woman thinks in her heart so she is," not only embraces the whole of a woman's being, but is so comprehensive as to reach out to every condition and circumstance of her life. A woman is literally what she thinks, her character being the complete sum of all her thoughts.

As the plant springs from and could not be without the seed, so every act of a woman springs from the hidden seeds of thought and could not have appeared without them. This applies equally to those acts called "spontaneous" and "unpremeditated" as to those, which are deliberately executed.

Act is the blossom of thought and joy

and suffering are its fruits; thus does a woman garner in the sweet and bitter fruit of her own life.

"Thought in the mind has made us, what we are by thought was wrought and built. If a woman's mind has bad thoughts, pain comes on her as comes the wheel the ox behind....   .

If one endures In purity of thought, joy follows her as her own shadow--sure."

Woman is a growth by law and not a creation by artifice and cause and effect is as absolute and undeviating in the hidden realm of thought as in the world of visible and material things. A noble and Godlike character is not a thing of favor or chance, but is the natural result of continued effort in right thinking, the effect of long cherished association with Godlike thoughts. An ignoble and bestial character, by the same process, is the result of the continued harboring of demeaning thoughts.

Woman is made or unmade by herself and in the armory of thought she forges the weapons by which she destroys herself and she also fashions the tools with which she builds for herself heavenly mansions of joy, strength and peace. By the right choice and true application of thought, woman ascends to the Divine Perfection; by the abuse and wrong application of thought, she descends below the level of the beast. Between these two extremes are all the grades of character and woman is their maker and master.

Of all the beautiful truths pertaining to the soul which have been restored and brought to light in this age, none is more gladdening or fruitful of divine promise and confidence than this--that woman is the master of thought, the moulder of character and the maker and shaper of her condition, environment and destiny.

As a being of Power, Intelligence and Love and the lord of her own thoughts, woman holds the key to every situation and contains within herself that transforming and regenerative agency by which she may make herself what she wills.

Woman is always the master, even in her weaker and most abandoned state, but in her weakness and degradation she is the foolish master who misgoverns her "household". When she begins to reflect upon her condition and to search diligently for the Law upon which her being is established, she then becomes the wise master, directing her energies with intelligence and fashioning her thoughts to fruitful issues. Such is the conscious master and woman can only thus become by discovering within herself the laws of thought; which discovery is totally a matter of application, self analysis and experience.

Only by much searching and mining are gold and diamonds obtained and a woman can find every truth connected with her being if she will dig deep into the mine of her soul and that she is the maker of her character, the moulder of her life and the builder of her destiny, she may unerringly prove if she will watch, control and alter her thoughts, tracing their effects upon herself, upon others and upon her life and circumstances, linking cause and effect by patient practice and investigation and utilizing her every experience, even to the most trivial, everyday occurrence, as a means of obtaining that knowledge of herself which is Understanding, Wisdom and

Power. In this direction, as in no other, is the law absolute that "She that seeks finds and to her that knocks it shall be opened;" for only by patience, practice and ceaseless importunity can a woman enter the Door of the Temple of Knowledge.

EFFECT OF THOUGHT ON CIRCUMSTANCES

WOMAN'S mind may be likened to a garden which may be intelligently cultivated or allowed to run wild; but whether cultivated or neglected, it must and will bring forth. If no useful seeds are put into it, then an abundance of useless weed seeds will fall therein and will continue to produce their kind.

Just as a gardener cultivates her plot, keeping it free from weeds and growing the flowers and fruits which she requires, so may a woman tend the garden of her mind, weeding out all the wrong, useless and impure thoughts and cultivating toward perfection the flowers and fruits of right, useful and pure thoughts. By pursuing this process, a woman sooner or later discovers that she is the master gardener of her soul, the director of her life.

She also reveals, within herself, the laws of thought and understands, with ever-increasing accuracy, how the thought forces and mind elements operate in the shaping of her character, circumstances and destiny.

Thought and character are one and as character can only manifest and discover itself through environment and circumstance, the outer conditions of a woman's life will always be found to be harmoniously related to her inner state. This does not mean that a woman's circumstances at any given time are an indication of her entire character, but that those circumstances are so intimately connected with some vital thought element within herself that, for the time being, they are indispensable to her development.

Every woman is where she is by the law

of her being; the thoughts which she has built into her character have brought her there and in the arrangement of her life there is no element of chance, but all is the result of a law which cannot err. This is just as true of those who feel "out of harmony" with their surroundings as of those who are contented with them.

As a progressive and evolving being, woman is where she is that she may learn that she may grow; and as she learns the spiritual lesson which any circumstance contains for her, it passes away and gives place to other circum- stances.

Woman is buffeted by circumstances so long as she believes herself to be the creature of outside conditions, but when she realizes that she is a creative power and that she may command the hidden soil and seeds of her being out of which circumstances grow, she then becomes the rightful master of herself.

That circumstances grow out of thought every woman knows who has for any length of time practiced self-control and self-purification; for she will have noticed that the alteration in her circumstances has been in exact ratio with her altered mental condition. So true is this that when a woman earnestly applies herself to remedy the defects in her character and makes swift and marked progress, she passes rapidly through a succession of vicissitudes.

The soul attracts that which it secretly harbours; that which it loves and also that which it fears; it reaches the height of its cherished aspirations; it falls to the level of its unchastened desires and circumstances are the means by which the soul receives its own.

Every thought-seed sown or allowed to fall into the mind and to take root there, produces its own, blossoming sooner or later into act and bearing its own fruit of opportunity and circumstance. Good thoughts bear good fruit, bad thoughts bear bad fruit.

The outer world of circumstance shapes itself to the inner world of thought and both pleasant and unpleasant external conditions are factors which make for the ultimate good of the individual. As the reaper of her own harvest, woman learns both by suffering and bliss.

Following the inmost desires, aspirations, and thoughts by which she allows herself to be dominated, (pursuing the will-o'-the-wisps of impure imaginings or steadfastly walking the highway of strong and high endeavour), a woman

at last arrives at their fruition and fulfil-
ment in the outer conditions of her life.
The laws of growth and adjustment ev-
erywhere obtains.

A woman does not come to the alms-
house or the jail by the tyranny of fate or
circumstance, but by the pathway of demeaning thoughts and base desires. Nor
does a pure minded woman fall suddenly
into crime by stress of any mere external force. The criminal thought had long
been secretly fostered in the heart and
the hour of opportunity revealed its gathered power. Circumstance does not make
the woman, it reveals her to herself. No
such conditions can exist as descend-
ing into vice and its attendant sufferings
apart from vicious inclinations, or as-
cending into virtue and its pure happiness without the continued cultivation of
virtuous aspirations and woman; therefore, as the lord and master of thought

is the maker of herself, the shaper and author of her environment. Even at birth the soul comes to its own and through every step of its earthly pilgrimage it attracts those combinations of conditions which reveal itself, which are the reflections of its own purity and impurity, its strength and weakness.

Women do not attract that which they want, but that which they are. Their whims, fancies and ambitions are thwarted at every step, but their inmost thoughts and desires are fed with their own food, be it foul or clean. The "divinity that shapes our ends" is in ourselves, it is our very self. Woman is only manacled by herself. Thought and action are the jailers of Fate--they imprison, being base; they are also the angels of Freedom--they liberate, being noble. Not what she wishes and prays for does a woman get, but what she justly earns.

Her wishes and prayers are only gratified and answered when they harmonize with her thoughts and actions.

In the light of this truth, what, then, is the meaning of "fighting against circumstances?" It means that a woman is continually revolting against an effect without, while all the time she is nourishing and preserving its cause in her heart. That cause may take the form of a conscious vice or an unconscious weakness; but whatever it is, it stubbornly slows the efforts of its possessor and thus calls aloud for remedy.

Women are anxious to improve their circumstances, but are unwilling to improve themselves; they therefore remain bound. The woman who does not shrink from self-crucifixion can never fail to accomplish the object upon which her heart is set. This is as true of earthly as of heavenly things. Even the woman whose sole object is to acquire wealth must be prepared to make great personal sacrifices before she can accomplish her object and how much more so she who would realize a strong and well-poised life?

Here is a woman who is wretchedly poor. She is extremely anxious that her surroundings and home comforts should be improved, yet all the time she shirks her work and considers she is justified in trying to deceive her employer on the ground of the insufficiency of her wages. Such a woman does not understand the simplest rudiments of those principles which are the basis of true prosperity and is not only totally unfitted to rise out of her wretchedness, but is actually attracting to herself a still deeper wretchedness by dwelling in and acting out, indolent, deceptive and unwomanly thoughts.

Here is a rich woman who is the victim of a painful and persistent disease as the result of gluttony. She is willing to give large sums of money to get rid of it, but she will not sacrifice her gluttonous desires. She wants to gratify her taste for rich and unnatural viands and have her health as well. Such a woman is totally unfit to have health, because she has not yet learned the first principles of a healthy life.

Here is an employer of labor who adopts crooked measures to avoid paying the regulation wage and in the hope of making larger profits, reduces the wages of her work people. Such a woman is altogether unfit for prosperity and when she finds herself bankrupt, both as regards reputation and riches, she blames circumstances, not knowing that she is the sole author of her condition.

I have introduced these three cases merely as illustrative of the truth that woman is the causer (though nearly always is unconsciously) of her circumstances and that, while aiming at a good end, she is continually frustrating its accomplishment by encouraging thoughts and desires which cannot possibly harmonize with that end. Such cases could be multiplied and varied almost indefinitely, but this is not necessary, as the reader can if she so resolves, trace the action of the laws of thought in her own mind and life and until this is done, mere external facts cannot serve as a ground of reasoning.

Circumstances; however, are so complicated, thought is so deeply rooted and the conditions of happiness vary so, vastly with individuals, that a woman's entire soul-condition (although it may be known to herself) cannot be judged by another from the external aspect of her life alone. A woman may be honest in certain directions, yet suffer privations; a woman may be dishonest in certain directions, yet acquire wealth, but the conclusion usually formed that the one woman fails because of her particular honesty and that the other prospers because of her particular dishonesty, is the result of a superficial judgment, which assumes that the dishonest woman is almost totally corrupt and the honest woman almost entirely virtuous. In the light of a deeper knowledge and wider experience such judgment is found to be erroneous. The dishonest woman may have some admirable virtues, which the other does not possess and the honest woman obnoxious vices which are absent in the other. The honest woman reaps the good results of her honest thoughts and acts. She also brings upon herself the sufferings which her vices produce. The dishonest woman likewise garners her own suffering and happiness.

It is pleasing to human vanity to believe that one suffers because of one's virtue, but not until a woman has extirpated every sickly, bitter and impure thought from her mind and washed every sinful stain from her soul, can she be in a position to know and declare that her sufferings are the result of her good and not of her bad qualities and on the way to, yet long before she has reached that supreme perfection, she will have found, working in her mind and life, the Great Law which is absolutely just and which cannot; therefore, give good for evil, evil for good. Possessed of such knowledge, she will then know, looking back upon her past ignorance and blindness, that her life is and always was, justly ordered and that all her past experiences, good and bad, were the equitable outworking of her evolving, yet unevolved self.

Good thoughts and actions can never produce bad results; bad thoughts and actions can never produce good results. This is but saying that nothing can come from corn, but corn, nothing from nettles, but nettles. Women understand this law in the natural world and work with it, but few understand it in the mental and moral world (though its operation there is just as simple and undeviating) and they; therefore, do not cooperate with it.

Suffering is always the effect of wrong thought in some direction. It is an indication that the individual is out of harmony with herself, with the Law of her being. The sole and supreme use of suffering is to purify, to burn out all that is useless and impure. Suffering ceases for her who is pure. There could be no object in burning gold after the dross had been removed and a perfectly pure and enlightened being could not suffer.

The circumstances, which a woman encounters with suffering, are the result of her own mental inharmony. The circumstances, which a woman encounters with blessedness, are the result of her own mental harmony. Blessedness, not material possessions, is the measure of right thought. Wretchedness, not lack of material possessions, is the measure of wrong thought. A woman may be cursed and rich, she may be blessed and poor. Blessedness and riches are only joined together when the riches are rightly and wisely used and the poor woman only descends into wretchedness when she regards her lot as a burden unjustly imposed.

Indigence and indulgence are the two extremes of wretchedness. They are both equally unnatural and the result of mental disorder. A woman is not rightly conditioned until she is a happy, healthy and prosperous being; and happiness, health and prosperity are the result of a harmonious adjustment of the inner with the outer, of the woman with her surroundings.

A woman only begins to be a woman when she ceases to whine and revile and commences to search for the hidden justice which regulates her life. And as she adapts her mind to that regulating factor, she ceases to accuse others as the cause of her condition and builds herself up in strong and empowering thoughts; ceases to kick against circumstances, but begins to use them as aids to her more rapid progress and as a means of discovering the hidden powers and possibilities within herself.

Law, not confusion, is the dominating

principle in the universe. Justice, not injustice, is the soul and substance of life and righteousness, not corruption, is the moulding and moving force in the spiritual government of the world. This being so, woman has but to right herself to find that the universe is right and during the process of putting herself right she will find that as she alters her thoughts towards things and other people, things and other people will alter towards her.

The proof of this truth is in every woman and it therefore admits of easy investigation by systematic introspection and self-analysis. Let a woman radically alter her thoughts and she will be astonished at the rapid transformation it will effect in the material conditions of her life. Women imagine that thought can be kept secret, but it cannot. It rapidly crystallizes into habit and habit solidifies into circumstance. Bestial thoughts crystallize into habits of drunkenness and sensuality, which solidify into circumstances of destitution and disease. Impure thoughts of every kind crystallize into enervating and confusing habits which solidify into distracting and adverse circumstances. Thoughts of fear, doubt and indecision crystallize into weak, unwomanly and irresolute habits which solidify into circumstances of failure, indigence and slavish dependence. Lazy thoughts crystallize into habits of uncleanliness and dishonesty which solidify into circumstances of foulness and beggary. Hateful and condemnatory thoughts crystallize into habits of accusation and violence which solidify into circumstances of injury and persecution. Selfish thoughts of all kinds crystallize into habits of self-seeking which solidify into circumstances more or less distressing. On the other hand, beautiful thoughts of all kinds crystallize into habits of grace and kindliness which solidify into genial and sunny circumstances. Pure thoughts crystallize into habits of temperance and self-control which solidify into circumstances of repose and peace. Thoughts of courage, self-reliance, and decision crystallize into womanly habits which solidify into circumstances of success, plenty, and freedom. Energetic thoughts crystallize into habits of cleanliness and industry which solidify into circumstances of pleasantness. Gentle and forgiving thoughts crystallize into habits of gentleness which solidify into protective and preservative circumstances. Loving and unselfish thoughts crystallize into habits of self-forgetfulness for others which solidify into circumstances of sure and abiding prosperity and true riches.

A particular train of thought persisted in; be it good or bad, cannot fail to produce its results on the character and circumstances. A woman cannot directly choose her circumstances, but she can choose her thoughts and so indirectly shape her circumstances.

Nature helps every woman to the gratification of the thoughts which she most encourages and opportunities are presented which will most speedily bring to the surface both the good and bad thoughts.

Let a woman cease from her sinful thoughts and all the world will soften towards her and be ready to help her; let her put away her weakly and sickly thoughts and lo, opportunities will spring up on every hand to aid her strong resolves; let her encourage good thoughts and no hard fate shall bind her down to wretchedness and shame. The world is your kaleidoscope and the varying combinations of colors, which at every suc-

ceeding moment it presents to you are
the exquisitely adjusted pictures of your
ever moving thoughts.

So You will be what you will to be;
Let failure find its false content
In that poor word, 'environment,'
But spirit scorns it, and is free.

It masters time, it conquers space;
It cows that boastful trickster, Chance,
And bids the tyrant Circumstance
Uncrown, and fill a servant's place.

The human Will, that force unseen,
The offspring of a deathless Soul,
Can hew a way to any goal,
Though walls of granite intervene.

Be not impatient in delays
But wait as one who understands;
When spirit rises and commands
The gods are ready to obey.

EFFECT OF THOUGHT
ON HEALTH AND THE BODY

THE body is the servant of the mind. It obeys the operations of the mind, whether they be deliberately chosen or automatically expressed. At the bidding of unlawful thoughts the body sinks rapidly into disease and decay and at the command of glad and beautiful thoughts it becomes clothed with youthfulness and beauty.

Disease and health, like circumstances, are rooted in thought. Sickly thoughts will express themselves through a sickly body. Thoughts of fear have been known to kill a man as speedily as a bullet and they are continually killing thousands of people just as surely though less rapidly. The people who live in fear of disease are the people who get it. Anxiety quickly demoralizes the whole body and lays it open to the entrance of disease while impure thoughts, even if not physically indulged, will soon shatter the nervous system.

Strong, pure and happy thoughts build up the body in vigor and grace. The body is a delicate and plastic instrument which responds readily to the thoughts by which it is impressed and habits of thought will produce their own effects, good or bad, upon it. Women will continue to have impure and poisoned blood, so long as they propagate unclean thoughts. Out of a clean heart comes a clean life and a clean body. Out of a defiled mind proceeds a defiled life and a corrupt body. Thought is the fount of action, life and manifestation; make the fountain pure and all will be pure.

Change of diet will not help a woman who will not change her thoughts. When

a woman makes her thoughts pure, she no longer desires impure food.
Clean thoughts make clean habits.
The so-called saint who does not wash her body is not a saint. She who has strengthened and purified her thoughts does not need to consider the malevolent microbe.

If you would protect your body, guard your mind. If you would renew your body, beautify your mind. Thoughts of malice, envy, disappointment, despondency, rob the body of its health and grace. A sour face does not come by chance, it is made by sour thoughts. Wrinkles that mar are drawn by folly, passion and pride.

I know a woman of ninety-six who has the bright, innocent face of a girl. I know a woman well under middle age whose face is drawn into inharmonious contours. The one is the result of a sweet and sunny disposition; the other is the outcome of passion and discontent.

As you cannot have a sweet and wholesome abode unless you admit the air and sunshine freely into your rooms, so a strong body and a bright, happy, or serene countenance can only result from the free admittance into the mind of thoughts of joy, goodwill and serenity.

On the faces of the aged there are wrinkles made by sympathy, others by strong and pure thought, and others are carved by passion. Who cannot distinguish them? With those who have lived righteously, age is calm, peaceful and softly mellowed, like the setting sun. I have recently seen a philosopher on his deathbed. She was not old except in years. She died as sweetly and peacefully as she had lived.

There is no physician like cheerful thought for dissipating the ills of the body. There is no comforter to compare with goodwill for dispersing the shadows of grief and sorrow. To live continually in thoughts of ill will, cynicism, suspicion and envy is to be confined in a self made prison cell. But to think well of all, to be cheerful with all, to patiently learn to find the good in all--such unselfish thoughts are the very portals of heaven; and to dwell day by day in thoughts of peace toward every creature will bring abounding peace to their possessor.

THOUGHT AND PURPOSE

UNTIL thought is linked with purpose there is no intelligent accomplishment. With the majority, the bark of thought is allowed to "drift" upon the ocean of life. Aimlessness is a vice and such drifting must not continue for her who would steer clear of catastrophe and destruction.

They who have no central purpose in their life fall an easy prey to petty worries, fears, troubles and self-pitying, all of which are indications of weakness, which lead, just as surely as deliberately planned sins (though by a different route), to failure, unhappiness and loss, for weakness cannot persist in a power evolving universe.

A woman should conceive of a legitimate purpose in her heart and set out to accomplish it. She should make this purpose the centralizing point of her thoughts. It may take the form of a spiritual ideal, or it may be a worldly object, according to her nature at the time being; but whichever it is, she should steadily focus her thought-forces upon the object, which she has set before her. She should make this purpose her supreme duty and should devote herself to its attainment, not allowing her thoughts to wander away into ephemeral fancies, longings and imaginings. This is the royal road to self-control and true concentration of thought. Even if she fails again and again to accomplish her purpose (as she necessarily must until weakness is overcome), the strength of character gained will be the measure of her true success and this will form a new starting point for future power and triumph.

Those who are not prepared for the apprehension of a great purpose should fix the thoughts upon the faultless performance of their duty, no matter how insignificant their task may appear. Only in this way can the thoughts be gathered and focussed and resolution and energy be developed, which being done, there is nothing which may not be accomplished.

The weakest soul, knowing its own weakness and believing this truth that strength can only be developed by effort and practice will, thus believing, at once begin to exert itself and adding effort to effort, patience to patience and strength to strength, will never cease to develop and will at last grow divinely strong.

As the physically weak woman can make herself strong by careful and patient training, so the woman of weak thoughts can make them strong by exercising herself in right thinking.

To put away aimlessness and weakness and to begin to think with purpose is to enter the ranks of those strong ones who only recognize failure as one of the pathways to attainment; who make all conditions serve them and who think strongly, attempt fearlessly and accomplish masterfully.

Having conceived of her purpose, a woman should mentally mark out a straight pathway to its achievement, looking neither to the right nor the left. Doubts and fears should be rigorously excluded; they are disintegrating elements, which break up the straight line of effort, rendering it crooked, ineffectual, useless. Thoughts of doubt and fear never accomplished anything and never can. They always lead to failure. Purpose, energy, power to do and all strong thoughts cease when doubt and fear creep in.

The will to do springs from the knowledge that we can do. Doubt and fear are the great enemies of knowledge and she who encourages them, who does not slay them, thwarts herself at every step.

She who has conquered doubt and fear has conquered failure. Her every thought is allied with power and all difficulties are bravely met and wisely overcome. Her purposes are seasonably planted and they bloom and bring forth fruit, which does not fall prematurely to the ground.

Thought allied fearlessly to purpose becomes creative force. She who knows this is ready to become something higher and stronger than a mere bundle of wavering thoughts and fluctuating sensations. She who does this has become the conscious and intelligent wielder of her mental powers.

THE THOUGHT FACTOR IN ACHIEVEMENT

ALL that a woman achieves and all that she fails to achieve is the direct result of her own thoughts. In a justly ordered universe, where loss of balance would mean total destruction, individual responsibility must be absolute. A woman's weakness and strength, purity and impurity, are her own and not another woman's; they are brought about by herself and not by another and they can only be altered by herself, never by another. Her condition is also her own and not another woman's. Her suffering and her happiness are evolved from within. As she thinks, so she is; as she continues to think, so she remains.

A strong woman cannot help a weaker unless that weaker is willing to be helped and even then the weak woman must become strong of herself. She must, by her own efforts, develop the strength which she admires in another. None, but herself can alter her condition.

It has been usual for women to think and to say, "Many women are slaves because one is an oppressor, let us hate the oppressor." Now, however, there is amongst an increasing few a tendency to reverse this judgment and to say, "One woman is an oppressor because many are slaves; let us despise the slaves."

The truth is that oppressor and slave are cooperators in ignorance and while seeming to afflict each other, are in reality afflicting themselves. A perfect Knowledge perceives the action of law in the weakness of the oppressed and the misapplied power of the oppressor. A perfect Love, seeing the suffering, which both states entail, condemns neither. A perfect Compassion embraces both oppressor and oppressed.

She, who has conquered weakness and has put away all selfish thoughts, belongs neither to oppressor nor oppressed. She is free.

A woman can only rise, conquer and achieve by lifting up her thoughts. She can only remain weak, and abject and miserable by refusing to lift up her thoughts.

Before a woman can achieve anything, even in worldly things, she must lift her thoughts above slavish animal indulgence. She may not, in order to succeed, give up all animality and selfishness by any means; but a portion of it must, at least, be sacrificed. A woman whose first thought is bestial indulgence could neither think clearly nor plan methodically, she could not find and develop her latent resources and would fail in any undertaking. Not having commenced to control her thoughts, she is not in a position to control affairs and to adopt serious responsibilities. She is not fit to act independently and stand alone. But she is limited only by the thoughts, which she chooses.

There can be no progress, no achievement without sacrifice and a woman's worldly success will be in the measure that she sacrifices her confused animal thoughts and fixes her mind on the development of her plans and the strengthening of her resolution and self-reliance. And the higher she lifts her thoughts, the more feminine, upright and righteous she becomes, the greater will be her success, the more blessed and enduring will be her achievements.

The universe does not favor the greedy, the dishonest, the vicious, although on the mere surface it may sometimes appear to do so, rather it helps the honest, the magnanimous, the virtuous. All the great Teachers of the ages have declared this in varying forms and to prove and know it a woman has but to persist in making herself more and more virtuous by lifting up her thoughts.

Intellectual achievements are the result of thought consecrated to the search for knowledge, or for the beautiful and true in life and nature. Such achievements may be sometimes connected with vanity and ambition, but they are not the outcome of those characteristics, then they are the natural outgrowth of long and arduous effort and of pure and unselfish thoughts.

Spiritual achievements are the consummation of holy aspirations. She who lives constantly in the conception of noble and lofty thoughts, who dwells upon all that is pure and unselfish, will, as surely as the sun reaches its zenith and the moon its full, become wise and noble in character and rise into a position of influence and blessedness.

Achievement, of whatever kind, is the crown of effort, the diadem of thought. By the aid of self-control, resolution, purity, righteousness and well directed thought a woman ascends; by the aid of animality, indolence, impurity, corruption and confusion of thought a woman descends.

A woman may rise to high success in the world and even to lofty altitudes in the spiritual realm and again descend into weakness and wretchedness by allowing arrogant, selfish and corrupt thoughts to take possession of her.

Victories attained by right thought can only be maintained by watchfulness. Many give way when success is assured and rapidly fall back into failure.

All achievements, whether in the business, intellectual, or spiritual world, are the result of definitely directed thought and are governed by the same law and are of the same method. The only difference lies in the object of attainment. She who would accomplish little must sacrifice little. She who would achieve much must sacrifice much. She who would attain highly must sacrifice greatly.

VISIONS AND IDEALS

THE dreamers are the saviors of the world. As the visible world is sustained by the invisible, so women, through all their trials and sins and sordid vocations are nourished by the beautiful visions of their solitary dreamers. Humanity cannot forget its dreamers; it cannot let their ideals fade and die; it lives in them; it knows them as the realities which it shall one day see and know.

Composer, sculptor, painter, poet, prophet, sage, these are the makers of the after world, the architects of heaven. The world is beautiful because they have lived; without them, laboring humanity would perish.

She who cherishes a beautiful vision, a lofty ideal in her heart, will one day realize it. Columbus cherished a vision of another world and he discovered it; Copernicus fostered the vision of a multiplicity of worlds and a wider universe and he revealed it; Buddha beheld the vision of a spiritual world of stainless beauty and perfect peace and he entered into it.

Cherish your visions; cherish your ideals; cherish the music that stirs in your heart, the beauty that forms in your mind, the loveliness that drapes your purest thoughts, for out of them will grow all delightful conditions, all heavenly environment; of these, if you but remain true to them your world will at last be built.

To desire is to obtain; to aspire is to achieve. Shall woman's basest desires receive the fullest measure of gratification and her purest aspirations starve for lack of sustenance? Such is not the Law:

such a condition of things can never obtain: "ask and receive."

Dream lofty dreams and as you dream, so shall you become. Your Vision is the promise of what you shall one day be; your Ideal is the prophecy of what you shall at last unveil.

The greatest achievement was at first and for a time a dream. The oak sleeps in the acorn; the bird waits in the egg; and in the highest vision of the soul a waking angel stirs. Dreams are the seedlings of realities.

Your circumstances may be uncongenial, but they shall not long remain so if you but perceive an Ideal and strive to reach it. You cannot travel within and stand still without. Here is a youth hard pressed by poverty and labor, confined long hours in an unhealthy workshop, unschooled and lacking all the arts of refinement. But she dreams of better things; she thinks of intelligence, of refinement, of grace and beauty. She conceives of, mentally builds up, an ideal condition of life; the vision of a wider liberty and a larger scope takes possession of her; unrest urges her to action and she utilizes all her spare time and means, small though they are, to the development of her latent powers and resources. Very soon so altered has her mind become that the workshop can no longer hold her. It has become so out of harmony with her mentality that it falls out of her life as a garment is cast aside and with the growth of opportunities, which fit the scope of her expanding powers, she passes out of it forever. Years later we see this youth as a full-grown woman. We find her a master of certain forces of the mind, which she wields with worldwide influence and almost unequalled power. In her hands, she holds the cords of gigantic responsibilities; she speaks and lo, lives are changed; men and women hang upon her words and remould their characters and sun-like, she becomes the fixed and luminous center round which innumerable destinies revolve. She has realized the Vision of her youth. She has become one with her Ideal.

And you, too, youthful reader will realize the Vision (not the idle wish) of your heart, be it base or beautiful, or a mixture of both, for you will always gravitate toward that which you, secretly, most love. Into your hands will be placed the exact results of your own thoughts; you will receive that which you earn; no more, no less. Whatever your present environment may be, you will fall, remain, or rise with your thoughts, your Vision, your Ideal. You will become as small as your controlling desire; as great as your dominant aspiration. In the beautiful words of Stanton Kirkham Davis, "You may be keeping accounts and presently you shall walk out of the door that for so long has seemed to you the barrier of your ideals and shall find yourself before an audience--the pen still behind your ear, the ink stains on your fingers and then and there shall pour out the torrent of your inspiration. You may be driving sheep and you shall wander to the city-bucolic and open-mouthed; shall wander under the intrepid guidance of the spirit into the studio of the master and after a time he shall say, 'I have nothing more to teach you.' And now you have become the master, who did so recently dream of great things while driving sheep. You shall lay down the saw and the plane to take upon yourself the regeneration of the world."

The thoughtless, the ignorant and the indolent, seeing only the apparent effects of things and not the things themselves, talk of luck, of fortune and chance. Seeing a woman grow rich, they say, "How lucky she is!" Observing another become intellectual, they exclaim, "How highly favored she is!" And noting the saintly character and wide influence of another, they remark, "How chance aids her at every turn!" They do not see the trials and failures and struggles which these women have voluntarily encountered in order to gain their experience and have no knowledge of the sacrifices they have made, of the undaunted efforts they have put forth, of the faith they have exercised that they might overcome the apparently insurmountable and realize the Vision of their heart. They do not know the darkness and the heartaches. They only see the light and joy and call it "luck". They do not see the long and arduous journey, but only behold the pleasant goal and call it "good fortune." They do not understand the process, but only perceive the result and call it chance.

In all human affairs there are efforts and there are results and the strength of the effort is the measure of the result. Chance is not. Gifts, powers, material, intellectual and spiritual possessions are the fruits of effort; they are thoughts completed, objects accomplished, visions realized.

The Vision that you glorify in your mind, the Ideal that you enthrone in your heart, this you will build your life by, this you will become.

SERENITY

CALMNESS of mind is one of the beautiful jewels of wisdom. It is the result of long and patient effort in self-control. Its presence is an indication of ripened experience and of a more than ordinary knowledge of the laws and operations of thought.

A woman becomes calm in the measure that she understands herself as a thought evolved being, for such knowledge necessitates the understanding of others as the result of thought and as she develops a right understanding and sees more and more clearly the internal relations of things by the action of cause and effect she ceases to fuss and fume and worry and grieve and remains poised, steadfast and serene.

The calm woman, having learned how to

govern herself, knows how to adapt herself to others; and they in turn, reverence her spiritual strength and feel that they can learn of her and rely upon her. The more tranquil a woman becomes, the greater is her success, her influence, her power for good. Even the ordinary trader will find her business prosperity increase as she develops a greater self-control and equanimity, for people will always prefer to deal with a woman whose demeanour is strongly equable.

The strong, calm woman is always loved and revered. She is like a shade-giving tree in a thirsty land, or a sheltering rock in a storm. "Who does not love a tranquil heart, a sweet-tempered, balanced life? It does not matter whether it rains or shines, or what changes come to those possessing these blessings, for they are always sweet, serene and calm. That exquisite poise of character, which we call serenity, is the last lesson of culture, the fruitage of the soul. It is precious as wisdom, more to be desired than gold--yes, than even fine gold. How insignificant mere money seeking looks in comparison with a serene life - a life that dwells in the ocean of Truth, beneath the waves, beyond the reach of tempests, in the Eternal Calm!

"How many people we know who sour their lives, who ruin all that is sweet and beautiful by explosive tempers, who destroy their poise of character and make bad blood! It is a question whether the great majority of people do not ruin their lives and mar their happiness by lack of self-control. How few people we meet in life who are well balanced, who have that exquisite poise which is characteristic of the finished character!

Yes, humanity surges with uncontrolled

passion, is tumultuous with ungoverned grief, is blown about by anxiety and doubt only the wise woman, only she whose thoughts are controlled and purified, makes the winds and the storms of the soul obey her.

Tempest-tossed souls, wherever you may be, under whatsoever conditions you may live, know this in the ocean of life the isles of Blessedness are smiling, and the sunny shore of your ideal awaits your coming. Keep your hand firmly upon the helm of thought. In the bark of your soul reclines the commanding Master; she does but sleep, wake Her. Self-control is strength, Right Thought is mastery, Calmness is power. Say unto your heart, "Peace, be still!"

This is the first of many personal development books that we will be offering. It seemed fitting to start with As a Woman Thinks because it is so very true

. If you think you can't do something, you're probably right and if you think you can, you're probably right again. Your mind and subconscious will go along with whatever story you decide to tell yourself and then come up with reasons to support this belief system you have created in your own mind.

We hope you have enjoyed As a Woman Think and we look forward to serving you again.

Live and Love with Passion!
Live Life Abundantly!
Our Love to You and Yours!
Janice & Mel

Please visit Life
Transformation Publishing at:
www.lifetransformationpublishing.com

and check out our other great titles.
New titles are being added frequently!